MW01244561

Mary L. Trump's

Too Much and

Never Enough

**How My Family Created the World's Most
Dangerous Man**

Intensive Life Publishing

Summary & Analysis

By

Blake Terry

Table of Contents

Note to Readers

This is an unofficial summary & analysis of Mary L. Trump's *Too Much and Never Enough: How My Family Created the World's Most Dangerous Man* designed to enrich your reading experience. Buy the original book by visiting the link or by scanning the QR code below.

https://link.intensivelife.com/TMNE

provided by this guide. The disclaimer applies to any damages or injury caused by the use and application, whether directly or indirectly, of any advice or information presented, whether for breach of contract, tort, neglect, personal injury, criminal intent, or under any other cause of action. You agree to accept all risks of using the information presented inside this book.

The fact that an individual or organization is referred to in this document as a citation or source of information does not imply that the author or publisher endorses the information that the individual or organization provided. This is an unofficial summary & analytical review and has not been approved by the original author of the book.

As a way of saying **THANK YOU**,

we are offering a **FREE** copy of *Summary of Untamed*.

You will also be part of our **mailing list**!

Just visit the link or scan the QR code below:

https://link.intensivelife.com/free

Too Much and Never Enough

Summary Overview

Released on July 14th, 2020, *Too Much and Never Enough: How My Family Created the World's Most Dangerous Man* is a revelatory tell-all book written by Mary L. Trump, a clinical psychologist with a Doctorate of Philosophy from the Derner Institute of Advanced Psychological Studies and niece of the 45th President of the United States—Donald J. Trump. The book, considered by various critics and reviewers as of a similar vein to John Bolton's *The Room Where It Happened*, paints a portrait of Donald Trump and the Trump family from an insider's perspective. Through this book, Mary Trump aims to shine a light on the dark history of the Trump family and seeks to explain how her uncle became the toxic man that currently occupies the White House.

Much of the book's content is written from Mary L. Trump's memory, from conversations and recorded interviews with other Trump family members, neighbors, various family friends and associates, as well as the use of legal documents, tax returns, private family journals and documents, correspondences, emails, photographs, and text to provide insight into events portrayed in the book. The smorgasbord of dysfunction of Donald Trump and the Trump family detailed in the book is clearly and uniquely brought forward and expertly analyzed by Mary, who is not only a primary Trump insider but also someone who has the educational background and grit to delve into a person's psychology. Through her accounts, we are urged to question not only the very nature of the man but also of the family that made him.

The book is subdivided into three parts that are also split into 14 chapters, a prologue, and an epilogue.

Chapter by Chapter Analysis

Prologue

The prologue begins with Mary's honest proclamation that as a kid growing up in the 1970s, she had always loved her last name. She recalls that at that time, the Trump name was not as well known outside of Brooklyn and Queens, yet she felt that her last name was her source of pride. She loved the way it sounded. She said that something about the name suited her as a tough and fearless six-year-old. Skip forward a decade in the 80s, as her uncle Donald began to expand the Trump family name's notoriety by plastering it all over his Manhattan business ventures, Mary's feelings about her family name and of her family begin to complicate. Mary proceeds to paint a clear picture of the duality of the prestige of the Trump name. She recalls an Amtrak train ride on

April 4th, 2017, on her way to a family dinner to celebrate her aunts Maryanne and Elizabeth's birthday in the White House. She mentions arriving into Union Station and passing a vendor with buttons for sale: The Trump family name—her last name and source of pride from childhood—in a red circle with a red slash through it: "DUMP TRUMP," "DEPORT TRUMP," and "TRUMP IS A WITCH." Conversely, upon arriving in the Trump International Hotel, which was accommodating the family that night, Mary comments on the clean and tasteful interiors and quips on how her last name was on everything from the shampoo, the conditioner, the slippers, the bathrobes, to even the wine—a complete juxtaposition of how her name was used earlier in the train station.

Mary then narrates meeting her relatives at the hotel before the birthday dinner. Her brother Fritz and his wife, aunt Maryanne, aunt Elizabeth, and her cousin Desmond are all present. She subtly bemoans that the only Trump sibling who would be missing from the celebration would be her father, Frederick Crist Trump, Jr.—the eldest son, fondly called Freddy. He had died 35 years prior. Once the family gathers, they are picked up by two White House Vans.

What follows is Mary's retelling of her emotions upon entering the White House. She mentions that she had never imagined that she would have had the opportunity to visit the White House, and especially not under the circumstance of her uncle being the President. As she crossed the White House halls, past life-sized portraits of former first ladies, Mary briefly stops in front of the portrait of Hillary Clinton and stands for a minute, completely silent—as if to process in herself that this has actually happened. Her uncle is the President of the United States, and she is about to meet him.

Emerging down the porticoes that line the path to the Oval Office, Mary can see her uncle sitting behind the Resolute desk. A meeting is ongoing with the Vice President, Speaker of the House, other congress members, and staffers gathered around Donald. The author mentions that the scene uncannily reminded her of her own grandfather's tactics at his Brooklyn office. Just like Donald, her grandfather would always have his people come to him, and they would be standing up while he remained seated. She further recalls how she experienced her grandfather's tactics first-hand. She mentions a memory from 1985. She was seeking permission to return to school to finish her degree, so she took her place standing in front of him and asked. Her grandfather looked at her and said, "That's stupid. Why would you do that for? Just go to trade school and become a reception-ist"—much to her annoyance.

Following the meeting, Mary narrates a brief and cold interaction she has with her cousin Eric, a small photo ses-sion with the whole family, and a short tour around the White House—notable from which is Donald's comment about how the White House has never looked better since George Washington lived in it—unaware that the house had not been opened 'til after George Washington had died.

After the tour, the family is ushered into the Executive Dining Room. There, the author narrates various curious and awkward interactions between family members—ranging from an awkward toast turned into a sort of campaign speech, Ivanka's grandstanding on her husband's arrival, and Donald dismissing Rob's remarks and embarrassing him. From these events, Mary provides us an examination of Don-ald Trump and the Trump family. She remarks that the last time the family had sat down for dinner together was for Fa-ther's Day in a Brooklyn restaurant many years ago, yet the same family dynamics play out again. One of the most striking retellings from this event is the speech that Donald makes about his daughter-in-law Lara, Eric's wife. He mentions that he had barely known who she was, but then she gave a great passionate speech in the State of Georgia for the campaign. At that time, Lara and Eric had been married for eight years, so presumably, Donald had at least met Lara at their wedding. But from his speech, it sounds as if he had never known who she was until she said good things about him. From this simple speech, Mary provides a glimpse into Donald's psyche—she mentions, "As usual with Donald, the story mattered more than the truth, which was easily sacrificed, especially if a lie made the story sound better."

The night was capped off with each Trump family member taking individual photos with Donald. When it was Mary's turn, she remarked that she could see the exhaustion behind her uncle's cheerful facade. Mary could visually see the toll the presidency had on her uncle. It was not long after the first cracks in Donald's presidency had started to show, and his first national security advisor had been removed in disgrace. "Don't let them get you down," she said to him. He responded, "They're not going to get me."

After recounting the events of that fateful dinner, Mary goes on to talk about the various conversations she had with her aunt Maryanne over their frequent lunches together about Donald's bid for the presidency. She mentions that when her uncle announced his run for the presidency on June 16th, 2015, none of the Trumps took it seriously. Mary believed Donald did not take it seriously either. It was all just free publicity for his brand, she believed. Maryanne Trump declared that Donald was a clown, and this would never happen—to which Mary agreed. Both Maryanne and Mary had believed that Donald's status as a failed businessman and washed-up reality star would ruin his campaign. However, his poll numbers continued to rise—much to Mary and Maryanne's surprise.

When Donald started addressing substance abuse by using Mary's dad Freddy's history with alcoholism to cement his anti-addiction agenda, Mary and Maryanne were outraged. The blatant racism on display during Donald's campaign rallies, his disparagement of his main political rival Secretary Clinton, and his insults addressed at a disabled New York Times reporter were no surprise to Mary. In fact, Mary relates that the Trump campaign of 2016 reminded her of every Trump family meal she had ever attended. During these meals, Donald would talk about all of the women he considered fat and ugly slobs, or the men that he saw as losers while the rest of her family would laugh and join in. She points out that dehumanization is commonplace at the Trump household. Though not surprised by her uncle's actions, what surprised Mary was his ability to get away with it. Not long after, her uncle would receive the Republican Party nomination—and all the things that would seem to disqualify him seemed only to appeal more to his core base.

At the same time, in the summer of 2016, the author considered speaking out about how she had known her uncle Donald to be completely incompetent and unqualified for the job. However, seeing as her uncle emerged untouched scandal after scandal—from the *Access Hollywood* tape, his hints at urging pro-gun individuals to assassinate Hillary Clinton, as well as his inherent racism towards Khizr Khan, whose son had died serving in Iraq—Mary began to realize that she was watching her family history and Donald's central role in it unfold on a national scale. Mary relates how Donald's competition in the race was being held to higher standards, similar to how his father had always been. However, Donald continued to get away with—and even rewarded for—horrible, vulgar, and irresponsible behavior. Mary laments that "This can't be happening again,"—but it was. She continues to point out that the media did not realize that at that point in the presidential race, not one member of the Trump family, apart from his children, his son-in-law, and his wife mentioned anything about supporting him. To the author, this is telling of Donald's complete unfitness for the office. Mary then begins to recount how growing up as Freddy's daughter presented certain difficulties in speaking out against Donald. She reveals that after her grandfather had passed away in 1999, she had learned that her father's line had completely been erased from the will as if her father had never existed—and an ugly lawsuit followed. Mary concluded that if she spoke publicly against her uncle, she would only be seen as a discontent and disinherited niece wanting to get even.

The author then begins the latter half of the prologue writing about what had brought Donald and the Trump family to this point—her grandfather. She believes that her grandfather's wanton need for notoriety had propelled Donald's recklessness and unearned confidence—which served to hide Donald's clinical weaknesses and insecurities. Mary mentions that as Donald was growing up, he was forced to cheer for himself to compete for his father's affection and prove that he was a better son than Freddy—because that was what his grandfather had expected of him. Mary then surmises that not long after, Donald started believing in his own hype as well, even if nobody else did. This made him address every difficulty with a sense of superiority and anger—as clearly played out during the election campaign. He believed in himself and had buried all his vulnerabilities so deep that he did not have to acknowledge they existed.

Mary then addresses the myth around Donald, who in the 1970s—after her grandfather had preferred to promote Donald over her father to helm the company—was eyed by the New York media. They began by picking up on Donald's hype and disseminating it. In the '80s, the banks joined in when they began funding his ventures. They were willing to foster Donald's increasingly unfounded claims to success even after a decade of fumbling, bankruptcies, and a series of failed products. Then, television producer Mark Burnett provided Donald another opportunity to expand his myth. "The Apprentice" sold the image of Donald as the brash, self-made dealmaker, the myth that Mary's grandfather had created, even as a vast trove of evidence showed otherwise. This persona of Donald would survive relatively unaltered and unscathed. By the time of Donald's nomination, most Americans had already been primed to believe his myth. Mary then boldly finishes this part of the prologue by pointing out that to this day, lies, fabrications, and delusions are the sum total of what makes her uncle Donald.

The author goes on to talk about how none of the Trump children has emerged unscathed from her grandfather's sociopathy and her grandmother's weakness but specifically points out that her father Fred and her uncle Donald had suffered the hardest. She declares that to get a clear psychological picture of Donald and his dysfunctional behavior, we need a thorough family history. She recounts watching all the pundits, journalists, and armchair historians calling her uncle a narcissist—and using phrases such as "malignant narcissism," "narcissistic personality disorder," and the like, in an attempt to make sense of Donald. Mary clarifies that she has no problem calling her uncle a narcissist—as he meets all the nine criteria outlined in the Diagnostic and Statistical Manual of Mental Disorders (DSM 5)—but she feels the label does not complete the story. She then continues by using her clinical psychology background to diagnose other things about her uncle and concludes that his pathologies are so complex and his behavior inexplicable that finding an accurate and comprehensive diagnosis would require a whole smorgasbord of psychological and neurological tests, something that her uncle would never be willing to partake in.

Mary closes out the prologue with an ominous realization and her reasoning for speaking up now and publishing her account. The author argues that "At the end of my aunts' birthday party in 2017, I could see that Donald was already under a kind of stress he'd never experienced before. As the pressures upon him have continued to mount over the course of the last three years, the disparity between the level of competence required for running a country and his incompetence has widened, revealing his delusions more starkly than ever before." She mentions that though most Americans have been protected and were largely unaffected until now by Donald's incompetence—that is no longer true. The COVID-19 pandemic has been out of control; the whispers of an economic depression, a stark political and racial divide within the country, and the devastating uncertainty about the country's future have all served as a catalyst for a catastrophe that, as Mary puts it, "no one is less equipped than my uncle to manage." Mary strongly contends that Donald's ability to control unfavorable situations by lying, manipulating, and bewilderment will prove impotent amid these challenges. She criticizes Donald's increasing antagonism against the level of scrutiny and push-back against him, and his need to enact petty revenge against those who do not brown-nose. She relates Donald to Mary Shelley's *Frankenstein* by citing a quote from the 1994 movie adaptation uttered by Frankenstein's monster, "I do know that for the sympathy of one living being, I would make peace with all. I have love in me the likes of which you can scarcely imagine and rage the likes of which you would not believe. If I cannot satisfy the one, I will indulge the other." As she points out, like Frankenstein's monster, Donald is Fred's—my grandfather's monster. Mary diagnoses that Fred's preference for Donald rendered him unlovable by everyone else. In the end, there would be no love that would satiate Donald at all, just a rage that would overshadow all.

It was the realization of her uncle's inept lack of capability to function and course-correct the current social situation, Mary's own familiarity with her uncle's true nature as part of the Trump family, and her perspective as a clinical psychologist that made her decide to speak up and write *Too Much and Never Enough*. Mary laments that she was seeing the atmosphere of division that her grandfather had created within the Trump family—on which Donald thrived, begin to wear the country down, just as it did to her father. And although the author mentions that her family might think that she is writing this book to cash in or out of spite and revenge, she argues that if that were the case, she would have written a book about the family years ago. However, recent events have forced her hand, and she can no longer remain silent.

Mary ends the prologue of her book with a hope and a goal. She encapsulates that *Too Much and Never Enough* is the story of the most powerful dysfunctional family and how specific events and general family patterns created the damaged man who currently occupies the Oval Office. Mary hopes that through her revelations, readers will understand how Donald Trump thinks and operates. Mary proclaims that Donald perpetuating the fantasies and fictions instilled by her grandfather, and by the inaction of the rest of the family, destroyed her father. And she cannot allow him to destroy her country.

Part 1: The Cruelty Is the Point

The first part of the book is titled "The Cruelty Is the Point." It comprises of four chapters and primarily focuses on the growing years of the Trump children and their relationships within the family. Each chapter slowly provides us a glimmer into how the Trumps grew up to be who they are.

Chapter 1: The House

Chapter 1, titled "The House," focuses on the childhood of the Trump children in their Queens home. In this chapter, Mary narrates the circumstances of the Trump children growing up and the underlying family dynamics at play in the Trump home. It begins with Maryanne, 12 at this time, discovering her mother bleeding and collapsed in their bathroom. She hurriedly gets her father, and they bring her unresponsive mother to the hospital. There, the doctors discover that Fred's wife has developed complications within her uterus, and in the span of the next six months, she undergoes two surgeries, being in and out of the hospital. From this point on, Maryanne's mother would always be physically weak and normally resigned to her room.

At this point, the author mentions that "As children, we need at least one emotionally available parent who could consistently fulfill our needs and respond to our desires for attention. Being held and comforted, having our feelings acknowledged and our upsets soothed are all critical for the healthy development of young children. This kind of attention creates a sense of safety and security that ultimately allows us to explore the world around us without excessive fear or unmanageable anxiety because we know we can count on the bedrock support of at least one caregiver." She elaborates that this is what is called Mirroring. In the author's own words, she connects the act of Mirroring in childrearing to the development of a person's empathy. She states that "Mirroring, the process through which an attuned parent reflects, processes, and then gives back to the baby the baby's own feelings, is another crucial part of a young child's development. Without mirroring, children are denied crucial information both about how their minds work and about how to understand the world. Just as a secure attachment to a primary caregiver can lead to higher levels of emotional intelligence, mirroring is the root of empathy."

After Mary emphasizes the importance of Mirroring and having the solid bedrock of support from our parents in the healthy growth of a child, she then urges the reader to correlate that with the Trump siblings, and their childhood growing up. She emphasizes that after their mother's surgeries, her absence created a void within the children's lives. The blow would have been especially hard for Donald, who, at two and a half at the time, was most vulnerable to the lack of a mother.

Mary then proceeds to talk about Fred Trump, her grandfather and Donald's father. She mentions that as Donald's mother was absent, Fred did not need an emotional connection with his children. She diagnoses Fred as a high-functioning sociopath. The author mentions that the symptoms of sociopathy, which include a lack of empathy, a facility for lying, indifference to right and wrong, abusive behavior, and a lack of interest in the rights of others, were prevalent within Fred. For Donald, having a sociopath as a parent, especially with no one else around to mitigate the effects, all but ensured the severe disruption in his ability to understand himself, regulate his emotions, and engage with the world. Since the Trump children's mother was emotionally and physically absent due to her injuries, Mary states that "Fred became, by default, the only available parent, but it would be a mistake to refer to him as a caregiver. He firmly believed that dealing with young children was not his job and kept to his twelve-hours-a-day, six-days-a-week job at Trump Management as if his children could look after themselves. He focused on what was important to him: his increasingly successful business." The author further elaborates that when his mother became ill and Donald's main source of comfort and connection was abruptly taken away, Fred was the only person left that he could depend on. However, Donald's needs were barely met at all by his father. That Fred would, by default, become the primary source of Donald's solace when he was much more likely to be a source of fear or rejection, put Donald into an intolerable position: being totally dependent on his father, who was also likely to be a source of his terror. Child abuse, as the author defines, is the experience of "too much" or "not enough"—and as for Donald, he experienced the "not enough" in the absence of his mother at his most crucial developmental stage, and his needs to be loved and valued were not met by his father. In the author's own words, she states that "Donald suffered deprivations that would scar him for life. The personality traits that resulted—displays of narcissism, bullying, grandiosity—finally made my grandfather take notice but not in a way that ameliorated any of the horrors that had come before. As he grew older, Donald was subjected to my grandfather's too-muchness: too much attention, too much expectation, and, most saliently, too much humiliation." As she puts it, it was her grandfather's uncaring behavior towards Donald that created his unlovable personality, and upon Donald becoming his father's center of attention when taking over the business instead of Freddy, Fred Trump came to validate, encourage, and champion the things about Donald that rendered him essentially unlovable.

Mary closes the chapter by continuing to talk about her grandfather's life. She mentions that Fred's focus was to further the successes of his financial empire and most of his actions revolved around this notion. Fred believed that financial worth was the same as self-worth; the monetary value was human value. For her grandfather, the more he had, the better off he was. If Fred Trump gave something to someone else, that person would be worth more, and he would be less. This line of thinking would be passed on to his son Donald.

Chapter 2: The First Son

The second chapter, titled "The First Son," focuses on the father-son dynamics between the author's grandfather and her father—Freddy Trump. The chapter also talks about how the former father-son relationship between Fred and Freddy would influence Donald growing up, as well as affect the relationship of the brothers.

The author begins the chapter by providing perspective on her father Freddy's position as the eldest son to Fred, and Fred's treatment of him. She mentions that Freddy's status as the eldest son was an immense and stressful burden. As Freddy got older, he became torn between the responsibilities that his father had placed on him and his natural inclination to live life his own way. By Freddy's teenage years, he understood that his future was held to what his father expected of him—and that he was not measuring up. In his early teens, Freddy started lying to his father about his life outside the house to avoid the mockery or disapproval he knew the truth would bring down on him. The author explains that for the Trump children, lying was a way of life. And for Freddy, lying was defensive. Compared to Maryanne, who lied as a way to circumvent her father's disapproval and avoid punishment, or Donald, who lied as a way of egoism meant to convince others that he was better than he actually was, Freddy's lies were to preserve his personality and a semblance of himself. For Freddy, the consequences of going against his father were different not only in degree but in kind, so lying became his only defense against his father's attempts to suppress his natural sense of humor, sensitivity, and adventure. For Fred Trump, weakness was the greatest sin of all, and this mindset helped shape his harsh judgments about his eldest son Freddy. Fred worried that his son would be weak and sought to change that. In the author's words, "Such softness was unthinkable in his namesake, and by the time the family had moved into the house when Freddy was ten, Fred had already determined to toughen him up. Like most people who aren't paying attention to where they're going, however, he overcorrected." Fred hated it when his oldest son screwed up or failed what was required of him. Fred would mock him. Fred wanted Freddy to be invulnerable because he was temperamentally the opposite of that. The author emphasizes that Fred didn't grasp that by ridiculing and questioning Freddy, he was creating a situation in which low self-esteem was almost inevitable. Fred was simultaneously telling his son that he had to be an unqualified success and that he never could be. So, Freddy existed in a system that was all punishment, no reward.

Mary then continues to elaborate that Donald could not help but notice Freddy's situation. The situation was different for him. With the benefit of a seven-and-a-half-year age gap, he had plenty of time to learn from watching Fred humiliate his older brother and Freddy's resulting shame. The lesson he learned, at its simplest, was that it was wrong to be like Freddy: Fred didn't respect his oldest son, so neither would Donald. Fred thought Freddy was weak, and so did Donald. To the author, Donald would have taken his father's treatment of his brother at face value: "Dad's not trying to hurt Freddy. He's only trying to teach us how to be real men. And Freddy's failing."

Mary then provides us a psychological perspective on what Freddy and Donald would have thought about the relationship they had with their father. She begins this by saying, "It's difficult to understand what goes on in any family—perhaps hardest of all for the people in it. Regardless of how a parent treats a child, it's almost impossible for that child to believe that parent means them any harm." With that, the author surmises that it would have been easier for Freddy to think that his father had his best interests at heart, and as such, Freddy was the problem. In other words, justifying his father's love was more important than protecting himself from abuse.

The author correlates the experiences of Freddy and Donald to abuse. In her own words, "Abuse can be quiet and insidious just as often as, or even more often than, it is loud and violent. As far as I know, my grandfather wasn't a physically violent man or even a particularly angry one. He didn't have to be; he expected to get what he wanted and almost always did. It wasn't his inability to fix his oldest son that infuriated him; it was the fact that Freddy simply wasn't what he wanted him to be. Fred dismantled his oldest son by devaluing and degrading every aspect of his personality and his natural abilities until all that was left was self-recrimination and a desperate need to please a man who had no use for him." To her, the only reason Donald had escaped the fate that beset Freddy was that his personality served his father's purpose. When Fred dismissed Freddy as a failure and changed his sights to Donald, he destroyed Donald too, but not by destroying his essence of personality, leaving a shell of self-loathing as he did with Freddy; instead, he perverted Donald and ramped up his personality, limiting Donald's access to his own emotions. Donald's capacity to be his own person would be lost, and all that would be left were the emotions and personality that allowed him to be an extension of his father's own ambitions. This inability to express a spectrum of emotion inhibited Donald and remained a constant buffer between him and his siblings. It also made reading social cues extremely difficult, if not impossible, for him—a problem he has to this day.

The chapter closes by exploring Freddy and Donald's relationships. Mary recalls Freddy, aged 14, dumping a bowl of mashed potatoes on Donald's head. This event had become a legend within the family, and it would hurt Donald's pride so deeply that he'd still be bothered by it when Maryanne brought it up in her toast at the White House birthday dinner in 2017. Donald had been tormenting Robert, the youngest of the Trump siblings, and nobody could get him to stop. Even at seven, he felt no need to listen to his mother, who, having failed to heal the rift between them after her illness, he treated with contempt. Finally, Robert's crying and Donald's needling became too much, and in a moment of improvised expedience that would become a family legend, Freddy picked up the first thing at hand that wouldn't cause any real damage: the bowl of mashed potatoes. Everybody laughed, and they couldn't stop laughing. And they were laughing at Donald. It was the first time Donald had been humiliated by someone he believed to be beneath him. He hadn't understood that humiliation was a weapon that could be wielded by more than one person in a fight. That Freddy, of all people, could humiliate him made it so much worse. This was Donald's first experience with humiliation, and he told himself that from then on, he would never allow himself to feel that feeling again. From then on, he would wield humiliation like a weapon, and never be at the sharp end of it.

Chapter 3: The Great I-Am

The following chapter, chapter 3, is titled "The Great I-Am," referring to a nickname Freddy gave Donald. The name itself echoes a passage in the book of Exodus in which God first reveals himself to Moses. It's supposed to be banter by Freddy on Donald's belief about his sense of superiority. The main focus of this chapter is Freddy's and Donald's coming-of-age. In this chapter, the author recalls Freddy's college years and subsequent time trying to fill his father's shoes, as well as Donald's teenage years of delinquency and his time at military school.

Mary begins the chapter by establishing Donald's personality and situation by the time Maryanne and Freddy had left for college. At this time, Donald had plenty of experience watching his older brother struggle with, and largely fail to meet, their father's expectations. It was one thing for Donald to stay out of his father's crosshairs and another to get into his good graces. To this end, Donald all but eradicated any qualities he might have shared with his older brother. He would become a creature of country clubs and offices. He would also double down on the behaviors he had thus far gotten away with: bullying, pointing the finger, refusing to take responsibility, and disregarding authority. In the author's words: "Donald says that he pushed back against his father and Fred respected that. The truth is, he was able to push back against his father because Fred let him. When he was very young, Fred's attention was not trained on him; his focus was elsewhere—on his business and his oldest son, that's it. Eventually, when Donald went away to military school at 13, Fred began to admire Donald's disregard of authority. Although a strict parent in general, Fred accepted Donald's arrogance and bullying—after he actually started to notice them—because he identified with the impulses." Encouraged by his father, and the attention he was receiving, Donald started believing his own hype. He was in a perpetual sneer of self-conscious superiority—ergo the nickname from Freddy— "The Great I-Am." The author then mentions that due to Donald's disastrous upbringing, he knew that no one would ever comfort and soothe him. His mother was too depleted, and Fred only cared about which-ever son could be of most use—so he became whatever was of most use. Whenever Freddy diverged from Fred's often implicit expectations, he ended up humiliated. Donald would try something different: he chose instead to ingratiate him-self with their father. He took what he wanted without ask-ing for permission not because he was brave but because he was afraid not to. Whether Donald understood the funda-mental message or not, Fred did: in family, as in life, there could be only one winner; everybody else had to lose. Freddy kept trying and failing to do the right thing; Donald began to realize that there was nothing he could do wrong, so he stopped trying to do anything "right." Eventually, this type of behavior would lead to him butting heads with his private school headmaster, as well as his mother who could not con-trol him at all. Any attempt at discipline was rebuffed. Fi-nally, by 1959, Donald's misbehavior had led him to be sent to the New York Military Academy. Fred went along with it. Throwing him in military school might toughen up Fred's burgeoning protégé even more. That September, Donald ar-rived at NYMA. He went from a world in which he could do as he wanted to one in which he faced punishment for the slightest insubordination. Fred recognized his son's isolation and visited almost every weekend between the time Donald started as an eighth-grader and the time he graduated in 1964. That somewhat mitigated Donald's sense of abandonment and grievance and gave him his first hopes that he had a connection with his father that his older brother did not.

As for Freddy, in college, his plans for the future still meant becoming his father's right-hand man, but while there, Freddy fell in love with flying, and his perspective shifted. Freddy thoughtfully planned out that as long as he finished his business major, he could fly, pledge into a fraternity, and join the US Air Force Reserve Officer Training Corps. And that's what he did. In college, as the author pointed out, Freddy found freedom. Being away from his father, Freddy was able to achieve and discover himself.

In 1960, Freddy officially joined his dad as part of Trump Management. There he would learn the importance of cost cuts and cost-saving. Fred dragged Freddy into Democratic Party meetings and introduced him to the most important and influential politicos in the city. While working for his father, Freddy started dating and married Linda Clapp. His father and mother assumed she must be a gold digger. After marriage, they moved in together in one of the Trumpmanaged buildings. There, they had their first son Frederick Christ Trump. Not long after, Freddy told Linda he wanted to be a commercial pilot. After three years at Trump Management, he found the work a grind. He mentioned to his wife that being a pilot would give him a chance to do something he loved while making a good living. His wife suggested shelving the idea first and making the best out of life at Trump Management. But the relationship between Freddy and his father continued to deteriorate. When Freddy approached him with ideas for innovation, Fred shot him down. When he asked for more responsibility, Fred brushed him off. Trying to prove he could make executive decisions, Freddy placed a window order for one of the older buildings. When Fred found out, he was furious. "Donald is worth ten of you. He never would have done anything so stupid," he shouted, while employees looked on. To Freddy, it was one thing for his father to humiliate him in front of his siblings, but the people in that office were employees. Someday, presumably, he would be their boss. For his nascent authority to be undermined so publicly, it felt like a body blow. That night, Freddy told his wife he felt trapped and confessed he'd never been happy working for his father. It wasn't at all what he had expected, and for the first time, it occurred to him that Trump Management might be a dead-end for him. "I'm applying to TWA, Linda. I have to." He wasn't asking anymore. Freddy did not care what his father would think of it. The author pointed out that, at this point, Freddy was willing to risk it all just to be free from his father.

The chapter closes with Freddy announcing to his father his intentions of leaving the company and becoming a commercial pilot. Fred was stunned. To him, it was a betrayal, and he had no intention of letting his eldest son forget it.

Chapter 4: Expecting to Fly

The fourth chapter, titled "Expecting to Fly," talks about Freddy's flying career after leaving Trump Management, as well as the subsequent repercussions of Freddy's decision.

The chapter starts with Mary recounting her family's move to Boston, and her father's employment with Trans World Airlines (TWA). She mentions that her dad was one of the few that were assigned the coveted Boston-Los Angeles route. Freddy seemed to be doing well for himself in his new profession. He had applied and was accepted in less than six months. Mary points out that what Freddy achieved in the cockpit made him unique in the Trump family. None of Fred's other children would accomplish much entirely on their own. Every other Trump sibling had some help from their dad or family connections. Maryanne received her appointment to a federal appeals court through Donald's connections. Elizabeth received her job at Chase Manhattan Bank through Fred's arrangements. As for Donald, he was enabled from the start, his very first projects funded and supported by Fred and then by myriad other enablers up to this day. Robert, after college, worked for the family. Only Freddy had put himself through flight school, defied Fred, and received the contempt of his family. He was determined, and he made it.

Freddy was not used to the prestige afforded to pilots. It was a welcome change from Trump Management, where he had struggled and failed to gain respect. Instead of having all his decisions being second-guessed by his father, on the flight deck, Freddy was in control. However, behind the scenes of Freddy's success were the constant barrages of abuse from his father in New York through letters and phone calls. To his father Fred, Freddy was nothing but a "bus driver in the sky." To Fred, Freddy's decision to leave Trump Management meant choosing failure. Due to constant abuse, Freddy began coping through drinking. Linda noticed this, yet Freddy did not confide in her anymore, wanting perhaps to shield her. Neither of them fully understood that to Freddy, his father's opinions mattered so much.

The chapter then continues to recall a visit Freddy and Linda had from Donald and Robert. It was about four months after Freddy had started flying. At the time of the visit, Donald was at a crossroads. When Freddy had announced he was stepping away from Trump Management in December 1963, Donald had no idea what his future role in the company might be. They had a barbecue for lunch, during which Donald told them he decided he was going to Chicago with their dad to "help" him with a development he was considering. Freddy's relief was palpable. Maybe Fred was beginning to accept the new reality and had decided to take Donald on as his heir apparent.

Later that day, they went fishing in Freddy's boat. Upon returning, a confrontation between Donald and Freddy erupted. "You know, Dad's really sick of you wasting your life." "I don't need you to tell me what Dad thinks," said Freddy, who already knew his father's opinions all too well. "Dad's right about you: you're nothing but a glorified bus driver," rebutted Donald. At that moment, Freddy understood that his brothers had been sent to deliver their father's message in person—or at least Donald had. But hearing Fred's belittling words come out of his little brother's mouth broke his spirit. Linda was rushing in to defend her husband, "You should just keep your mouth shut, Donald! Do you know how hard he's had to work? You have no idea what you're talking about!" Freddy didn't speak to either of his brothers for the remainder of that night, and they left for New York the next morning, a day earlier than planned.

Freddy's alcoholism worsened.

The author then points out the grim reality that Freddy had begun to realize that his dream was a failure. His father would never accept him as a professional pilot, and without that acceptance, he probably couldn't continue. He had spent his entire life up until he had left Trump Management trying his best to become the person his father wanted him to be. When those attempts had repeatedly failed, he had hoped that in the course of fulfilling his own dream, his father would come to accept him for who he really was. He had spent his childhood navigating the minefield of his father's conditional acceptance, and he knew all too well that there was only one way to receive it—by being someone he wasn't—and he would never be able to pull that off.

A few weeks after his brothers' visit, Freddy quit his job with TWA and moved back to New York. His drinking was out of control, and with no other options, he found himself standing in front of his father, asking for a job that he didn't want and Fred didn't think he could do. Fred reluctantly agreed, making it clear that he was doing his son a favor.

The only self-made man in the family was being slowly, inexorably dismantled.

Part 2: The Wrong Side of the Tracks

The second part of the book is titled "The Wrong Side of the Tracks." It comprises of four chapters and primarily focuses on the juxtaposition of Freddy's and Donald's lives as they navigate the world of adulthood and working for their father in Trump Management.

Chapter 5: Grounded

Chapter 5, "Grounded," focuses on Freddy's life after returning into Trump Management, as well as Donald's college days in the Wharton School in Pennsylvania.

The author begins the chapter by narrating Donald's attempts to get into the Wharton School of the University of Pennsylvania. Unfortunately, Donald's GPA was subpar, and he worried that this would scuttle his efforts. As such, he enlisted Joe Shapiro, a smart kid with a reputation for being a good test taker, to take his SATs for him. He also enlisted James Nolan, a Pennsylvania University admissions officer, to put in a good word for him. In the end, all of Donald's machinations succeeded. Donald got what he wanted. In the fall of 1966, his junior year, he would be admitted into the University of Pennsylvania.

As for Freddy, he was assigned by Fred to helm the recent acquisition of Steeplechase Park in Coney Island. However, nothing had changed since his previous stint at Trump Management. Fred's constant micromanaging and lack of respect for his son made what could have been an exciting challenge a grim, joyless exercise. Failure, it went without saying, would have been a disaster. Freddy still believed, though, that if he had a hand in pulling the development off, he'd be on a much better footing with his father. As the project went underway, there was considerable push-back from the locals. Trump Management plans for Steeplechase were in peril. Nevertheless, Fred made Freddy responsible for the nearly impossible task of making Steeplechase a success. Time was running out. Suddenly, Freddy, at 28, had a more public role, giving press conferences and arranging photo ops. In a last-ditch effort, Fred decided to host an event to celebrate the park's demolition. He had Freddy do the publicity and media press conferences, making him the face of the controversy.

The spectacle was a disaster.

Due to a local rebellion against his project, Fred was unable to secure the zoning change he needed and was forced to back out of the Steeplechase development. Unable to accept responsibility, much as Donald would later be, Fred blamed Freddy for the failure of Steeplechase. Eventually, Freddy blamed himself. Mary then narrates to us a confrontation between Fred, Freddy, and Donald in the breakfast room of the Trump family home after the failure of the Steeplechase venture. Fred was acrimonious and accusatory, and Freddy was defensive and remorseful. Donald casually said to his brother, as though completely unaware of the effect his words would have, "Maybe you could have kept your head in the game if you didn't fly out to Montauk every weekend." Freddy's siblings knew that their father had always disapproved of what was now merely Freddy's hobby. There was a tacit agreement that they wouldn't talk about the planes or the boats in front of the Old Man. Fred's reaction to Donald's revelation proved the point when he said to Freddy, "Get rid of it." The next week, the plane was gone. Freddy was grounded.

The next two years for Freddy would be marred with bouts of pneumonia and alcoholism. Linda would see her husband deteriorate while working for Trump Management. Freddy tried as best he could to revive his passion. However, every time Fred would find out about a new plane, a new boat, and cabin trips to Montauk, he put a stop to it.

Chapter 6: A Zero-Sum Game

Chapter 6, "A Zero-Sum Game," referring to Fred and Donald's outlook on life—that they had all to gain, and everyone else had all to lose, narrates the events of Donald's first year working for Trump Management and the continuing downward spiral of Freddy's life.

Mary opens the chapter with a memory from her childhood; she's awoken in the middle of the night by her father's maniacal laughter. She witnesses her drunken father pointing a rifle at her mother. Her mother manages to escape and take her and her brother away that night. The following day, Freddy is remorseful and promises that it will never happen again. The couple tries to work it out. However, a few months later, they are divorced, and her father is left with nothing but contempt from all sides of the family.

As for Donald, after graduating from the University of Pennsylvania in the spring of 1968, he goes straight to working at Trump Management. From his first day on the job, Mary's 22-year-old uncle is given more respect and perks and paid more money than Freddy ever had been. Almost immediately, Fred appoints Donald vice president of several companies that fell under the Trump Management umbrella, names him "manager" of a building he didn't actually have to manage, gives him "consulting" fees, and "hires" him as a banker.

The reasoning for that was twofold: first, it was an easy way to put Freddy in his place while signaling to the other employees that they were expected to defer to Donald. Second, it helped consolidate Donald's de facto position as heir apparent. Fred exposed his younger son to the ins and outs of the real estate business. Donald discovered he had a taste for the seamier side of dealing with contractors and navigating the political and financial power structures that undergirded the world of New York City real estate. Father and son could discuss the business and local politics and gossip endlessly. Not only did Fred and Donald share traits and dislikes, but they also had the ease of equals, something Freddy could never achieve with his father.

Everything considered, Donald's bid to replace Freddy as successor at Trump Management was off to a strong start.

Chapter 7: Parallel Lines

Chapter 7, titled "Parallel Lines," talks about the rise of Donald's business in Manhattan and Freddy's bouts with alcoholism and attempts to find hope within his life. The title refers to the parallels between Donald's and Freddy's lives and the ironic difference in their eventual trajectories.

The author begins the chapter by pointing out that when Freddy (in 1960) and Donald (in 1968) joined Trump Management, each had a similar expectation: to become his father's right-hand man and then succeed. However, the similarities ended there. Freddy quickly found that his father was unwilling to make room for him or delegate him any but the most mundane tasks. As for Donald, he was promoted, then only 24, to the position of president of Trump Management. He'd been on the job for only three years and had very little experience and even fewer qualifications, but Fred didn't seem to mind. Mary believed that the main purpose of Donald's promotion was to humiliate Freddy. Fred was determined to find a role for Donald. He had begun to realize that although his middle son didn't have the temperament for the day-to-day attention to detail that was required to run his business, he had something more valuable: bold ideas and the boldness to realize them.

Mary states that besides being driven around Manhattan by a driver in a Cadillac, Donald's job description seemed to have included lying and dedicating a significant portion of his time to crafting an image for himself among the Manhattan circles he was desperate to join. Despite Donald having done nothing for a myriad of developments for Trump Management, he was still paid handsomely, and Fred ensured that he got all the credit as well. By the time Donald had married, he had acquired a ten-million-dollar penthouse in the heart of Manhattan. Fred knew that anything his son got credit for would redound to his own benefit. After all, if Donald was embraced as an up-and-coming dealmaker, that was entirely to the credit of Fred Trump—even if Fred was the only person who knew it.

At the same time, Fred had taken Freddy's dream of flying away from him, and he had now lost his birthright. He was divorced and barely saw his children. He had no idea what was left for him. Whatever he had, Freddy knew all too well he was at Fred's mercy.

Chapter 8: Escape Velocity

The eighth chapter of the book is titled "Escape Velocity" and narrates the end of Freddy's life, the Trump family's reactions to losing Freddy, as well as the author's own experiences as a 16-year-old losing her father.

Freddy's bouts with alcoholism had left him very sick. He had moved back with his parents after being diagnosed with a heart defect. Mary described her father as not-yet-40, yet looking like a worn-out 80-year-old. Freddy had lost his home and family, his profession, much of his willpower, and most of his friends. Eventually, his parents were the only people left to take care of him. And they resented it. In the end, Freddy's very existence infuriated Fred. Mary pointed out that "Fred's treatment of my father had always served as an object lesson to his other children—a warning. In the end, though, the control became something much different.

Fred wielded the complete power of the torturer, but he was ultimately as trapped in the circumstance of Freddy's growing dependence due to his alcoholism and declining health as Freddy was tied to him."

At the age of 16, Mary started boarding school. Unknown to her at the time, as she was settling in at her new school, her father had already been severely weak for a month. In Mary's own words, "September 26th, 1981, one of my grandparents called an ambulance. I didn't know it then, but my father had been critically ill for three weeks. It was the first time anybody had called for medical help."

That night, at 9:20 p.m., Freddy was dead.

At the wake, Mary narrates her brother's eulogy for her father. She mentions that her brother reminisced about the good times he and his dad had had together, most of which had occurred before Mary had been old enough to remember them, but he refused to shy away from the fundamental reality of Freddy's life. At one point, he referred to his dad as the black sheep of the family, and there were audible gasps from the guests. Mary recalled that she felt a thrill of recognition and a sense of vindication—at long last. Her brother, who had always been so much better at negotiating the family than Mary was, had dared tell the truth. Mary admired his honesty but also felt jealous that he seemed to have so many more good memories of her father than she did.

The house seemed to grow colder as Mary got older. The first Thanksgiving after her father died, the house felt colder still.

As for Fred and Donald, they acted as if nothing was different. Their son and brother was dead, but they discussed New York politics, deals, and ugly women, just as they always had.

Part 3: Smoke and Mirrors

The third part of the book is titled "Smoke and Mirrors." It comprises of four chapters and primarily focuses on the events after Freddy's death, Fred's later life, and Donald's financial ventures and eventual failures.

Chapter 9: The Art of the Bailout

Chapter 9, titled "The Art of the Bailout," focuses on Donald's financial floundering in the 1980s and '90s, and exposes him not as the dealmaker his reputation was built upon but as a real estate blunderer who does not know anything about what he is doing. It also recounts the author's own college life and her eventual enlistment as Donald's ghostwriter.

Donald's alleged success with the Grand Hyatt in 1980 had paved the way for Trump Tower, which opened to much notoriety in 1983.

It was reported that Donald had treated the undocumented workers who built it poorly and that there was alleged Mob involvement; the project was marred in controversy. The outrage culminated in the destruction of the beautiful Art Deco of the Bonwit Teller Building, which Donald razed to make room for his own structures. When confronted about this, Donald shrugged it off and declared the structure to have no "artistic merit," as if he knew better. In the author's own words, she mentions how this event would characterize Donald's current penchant for believing only what he himself thinks. She says, "Over time, that attitude—that he knew better—would become even more entrenched: as his knowledge base has decreased (particularly in areas of governing), his claims to know everything have increased in direct proportion to his insecurity, which is where we are now."

However, the author discloses that the true reason Donald's first two projects succeeded was in large part thanks to Fred's ability as a developer and dealmaker. Before that point, Donald had relied entirely on Fred's money and influence—although he never acknowledged it and credited his own wealth and intellect for his success. The news media were more than happy to accept Donald's statements as fact, and the banks followed suit.

Soon, Donald was setting his sights on the casino scene in Atlantic City, New Jersey. In the interest to gain some influence in the state he was about to do a lot of business, Donald tugged on some strings to have his sister Maryanne appointed to the US District Court for the District of New Jersey. If Fred's opinion had carried any weight with him, Donald would never have invested in Atlantic City. Manhattan had already been a risk, however with this new venture— there would be no knowledge of the industry to draw upon. By then, it was evident Fred's influence over him was waning.

By 1985, Donald had purchased two casinos in Atlantic City and had gone all-in on his perceived idea that Atlantic City had unlimited potential. By 1990, his ventures would carry a billion dollars in debt. Even so, that same year, he purchased Mar-a-Lago for eight million dollars, a yacht, an airline for 365 million dollars, and issued over seven hundred million dollars in shady bonds to complete his third casino, the Taj Mahal. In the author's own words, "It seemed like the sheer volume of purchases, the price tags of the acquisitions, and the audacity of the transactions kept everybody, including the banks, from paying attention to his fast-accumulating debt and questionable business acumen." The banks were bleeding money. Just as the Taj was opening, Donald and his lenders were meeting to try to figure out how to rein in and manage his spending. The possibility of defaults and bankruptcies still loomed. He was legally obligated to pay the banks back, and if he didn't, there would be consequences. At least there should have been. However, despite restrictions, Donald kept spending cash he did not have. Donald, hemorrhaging money, fully believed what was happening to him was the result of a poor US economy, bad treatment by the banks, and bad luck. This was one of Donald's highlight traits—deflecting responsibility.

While Donald was floundering in Atlantic City, Mary had just recently completed her master's degree. While she was staring at the traffic outside her studio apartment window, she received a call from her uncle Donald. He had read one of Mary's write-ups sent to him by the dean of the college Mary had gone to. Donald said, "Do you want to write my next book? The publisher wants me to get started, and I thought it would be a great opportunity for you. It'll be fun."

Mary jumped at the opportunity.

The second half of the chapter talks about Mary following Donald around while trying to get material for the book

Donald wanted to publish. The book's title was *The Art of the Comeback*—referring to Donald's miraculous save of his current financial situation. However, as Mary points out, "I set about trying to explain how, under the most adverse circumstances, he had emerged from the depths, victorious and more successful than he had ever been. There wasn't much evidence to support that narrative—he was about to experience his fourth bankruptcy filing with the Plaza Hotel—but I had to try." This was the condition in which Mary had to write.

Mary followed Donald around and was even a guest at Mar-a-Lago for a weekend. She struggled with getting Donald to sit down for an interview. And yet, the progress was made. She sourced information from managers of Donald's casinos, employees, and such.

After a few months of working as Donald's ghostwriter, Donald told Mary that his editor wanted to speak with her. A lunch was set up wherein Mary thought they would discuss the next steps of the book. However, with very little preliminary conversation, the editor told her she was fired. Donald had someone else fire his niece for him.

Mary ends the chapter by mentioning that she did not feel bad about being fired. She states that even after all of the time she had spent in the office, she still did not know what Donald actually did.

Chapter 10: Nightfall Does Not Come at Once

Chapter 10, titled "Nightfall Does Not Come at Once," focuses on Fred's slow descent into dementia, his bout with Alzheimer's, and the later days of his life.

The chapter opens with Fred, Mary, and Maryanne, sitting on the pool deck at Mar-a-Lago. Fred says: "Isn't she a nice lady," referring to Mary. "Yes, Dad," Maryanne replies while smiling wearily. He had already forgotten who Mary was and had begun referring to her as the "nice lady." After, he looked at Maryanne carefully and, almost as an afterthought, asked, "Who are you?" Her eyes watered as if somebody had slapped her. "Dad," she said gently, "it's Maryanne." "Okay, Maryanne." He smiled, but the name didn't mean anything to him anymore.

Fred began forgetting words and misplacing things. Soon enough, he was forgetting familiar faces. Mary mentions that you could measure your worth in Fred's eyes by how long he remembered you. He had forgotten Mary, Maryanne, Elizabeth, Fritz, and Robert, but he never forgot Donald.

However, Donald had given up all pretense of caring about what his father thought or wanted. Donald would just shrug off his old man's request and advice. Having served his father's purpose, Donald now treated him with contempt, as if his mental decline were somehow his own fault.

Fred had spent his life worried constantly about money, terrified that his fortune was disappearing. Fred had never been poor a day in his life, but poverty became his sole preoccupation; he was tortured by the prospect of it.

Now, he was losing his memory.

On June 11th, 1999, Fred was hospitalized. Everyone in the Trump family thought it was likely the end. He died on the 25th.

Chapter 11: The Only Currency

Chapter 11, with the title "The Only Currency," talks about the aftermath of Fred's death for the Trump family, the execution of his will, and the division of his estate.

The chapter begins with Mary receiving a DHL package containing a copy of her grandfather's will. She checked through it twice to make sure.

She called up her brother Fritz and explained to him the situation. "So, what's the deal?" he asked. "Nothing," Mary told him. "We got nothing."

Over the course of the next three months, Mary and her brother Fritz would meet with their uncle Robert to discuss the contents of the will. Robert acted as if everything was alright and urged the siblings to sign so the will could be executed. The will seemingly disinherited Mary and her brother—that is, instead of splitting what would have been Mary's father's 20% share of Fred's estate between Mary and Fritz, Fred had divided it evenly among his four other children.

"Cash in your chips, Honeybunch," Rob frequently said during their meetings. The will couldn't go to probate until all of the beneficiaries had signed off. Mary and Fritz refused to do so until they knew exactly what was going on. Eventually, Rob's patience began waning. "Listen, your grandfather didn't give a shit about you," he said to them. "It's pretty simple," he said. "As far as your grandfather was concerned, dead is dead."

Everything seemed cordial at the start. Fritz, Robert, and Mary even agreed that they would leave Mary's grandmother out of it. However, as Mary lost track of how many meetings the three had in the span of three months, headway was not made between them, and after consulting their attorneys, Mary and Fritz decided to sue.

"Your grandfather didn't want you or Fritz, or especially your mother, to get anything," Rob said while on the phone with Mary. She took a deep breath. "This is going nowhere,"

Mary said. "Fritz and I are going to hire an attorney." As if a switch had been flipped, Robert screamed, "You do whatever the fuck you need to do!" and slammed the phone down.

The next day, Mary receives a call from her grandmother. "Your uncle Robert tells me you and your brother are suing for twenty percent of your grandfather's estate," her grandmother said. Mary felt blindsided. Rob had broken their agreement and told her grandmother his version of what was being discussed. Her grandmother spoke as if Mary getting what would have been her father's portion of the estate was somehow wrong. Mary was confused. She thought she was part of the family. She was treated as if she was not. "We're just trying to figure this out, that's all," Mary replied.

Chapter 12: The Debacle

Chapter 12, titled "The Debacle," talks about the lawsuit filed by Mary and Fritz against their grandfather's estate as well as their falling-out with the family.

Mary and Fritz approached Jack Barnosky, a partner at Farrell Fritz, who agreed to take them on as his clients. Their strategy was to prove that my grandfather's 1990 will should be overturned: Fred Trump had not been of sound mind at the time the will was signed, and he had been under the undue influence of his children. The lawsuit trials immediately became ugly. Robert reiterated Mary's grandfather's hatred of her mother as his central justification for the disinheritance; Maryanne angrily referred to Mary and her brother as "absentee grandchildren." All three of them claimed in their sworn depositions that my grandfather had been "sharp as a tack" until just before he died.

After almost two years, with legal bills piling up and having made no progress on any kind, reluctantly, Mary and Fritz decided to settle.

While the lawsuits were ongoing, Mary's grandmother had gone sick and died on August 7th, 2000. Mary laments, "If I had known she was sick, I think I would have tried to see her, but the fact that she hadn't asked to see me clarified just how easy it had been for us to let each other go." They never spoke after their last conversation over the phone.

Mary received a copy of her grandmother's will a few weeks after she died. It was a carbon copy of her grandfather's, with one exception: Freddy and his entire line had now been effectively erased.

Part 4: The Worst Investment Ever Made

Part 4 of the book, titled "The Worst Investment Ever Made," is composed of two chapters and primarily speaks about events after the lawsuit, Donald's presidency, and a thorough diagnosis of his psyche.

Chapter 13: The Political Is Personal

Chapter 13, titled "The Political Is Personal," talks about Mary's subsequent reunion with the rest of the family ten years after the settlement of the suit, as well as her assistance in exposing hundreds of millions of dollars in tax fraud.

Mary begins the chapter by recalling Ivanka and Jared's marriage in 2009. She was surprised that she was even invited. During the wedding, Mary spoke to her aunts and uncles and effectively made up with them. As Rob put it, "the statute of limitations on family estrangement has passed." Following a ten-year estrangement, Mary began to have lunches with her aunt Maryanne. She said that this was the first time after her grandmother that she had gotten close to a family member.

Mary then brings us to 2017, a couple of months after Maryanne's birthday in the White House, a reporter from the New York Times by the name of Susanne Craig contacted her at her home. She said that Mary possessed documents from the lawsuit that could, as she put it, "rewrite the history of the President of the United States." At first, Mary refused to cooperate; however, upon seeing the state of affairs in the United States in the succeeding months, she relented and assisted. With Mary's assistance, Susanne Craig and her colleagues Russ Buettner and David Barstow exposed a long litany of potentially fraudulent and criminal activities Mary's grandfather, aunts, and uncles had engaged in. This was contained in a 14-thousand-word article in the New York Times.

Chapter 14: A Civil Servant in Public Housing

Chapter 14, titled "A Civil Servant in Public Housing," focuses on the author's psycho-analysis of Donald. Using her insider perspective as a family member as well as her background in clinical psychology, she draws a final diagnosis of Donald trump's psyche.

The author states at the start of the chapter, a returning theme throughout the entirety of the book—Donald Trump was the creation of her grandfather. He was a product of "never enough" love and acknowledgment by his father at the beginning of his life, and "too much" attention once he became Fred's vanity project. Fred had taken advantage of Donald and used his aberrant personality, focused and exacerbated it till nothing was left.

The author claims that the Donald today is much as he was at three: incapable of growing, learning or evolving, unable to regulate his emotions, moderate responses, or take in and synthesize information. A product of "never enough," his deep-seated insecurities have created in him a black hole of need that constantly requires the light of compliments that disappears as soon as he's soaked it in. The author proclaims that this is far beyond garden-variety narcissism.

The author also points out that from his childhood in the house to his early forays into the New York real estate world and high society to today, Donald's aberrant behavior has been consistently normalized by others. His "skills" of self-aggrandizement, lying, and sleight of hand were identified and focused on by Fred as strengths unique to his brand of success.

The chapter ends with the author surmising, "This is the end result of Donald's having continually been given a pass and rewarded not just for his failures but for his transgressions—against tradition, against decency, against the law, and against fellow human beings."

Epilogue: The Tenth Circle

Too Much and Never Enough closes with an epilogue titled "The Tenth Circle." It presents the author discussing the current state of affairs within American society and how Donald is handling it. Mary laments the fact that America has turned into a grand version of the Trump family. She underscores Donald's attempts to minimize negativity at all costs amid the COVID-19 pandemic. She mentions the irony in which Donald's attempts to avoid the truth will inevitably cause the loss of hundreds of thousands of lives, and the economy of the richest country in the world may well be destroyed. She bemoans the fact that instead of action, Donald withdraws to his comfort zones—Twitter, Fox News, and casting blame.

The book closes with the author proclaiming that the country is now suffering from the same toxicity that her grandfather had developed to torment his first-born son and damage—beyond repair—the psyche of his favorite child, Donald J. Trump.

About *Too Much and Never Enough: How My Family Created the World's Most Dangerous Man*

Published in July 2020, *Too Much and Never Enough: How My Family Created the World's Most Dangerous Man* is a controversial tell-all book by Mary L. Trump, niece of President Donald J. Trump. The book attempts to shine a light on various events within the Trump family with the goal of explaining how Donald Trump became the person he is. The book also tries to provide a thorough psychological analysis of Donald Trump's psyche, upbringing, and relationships through the author's clinical psychology background.

Too Much and Never Enough: How My Family Created the World's Most Dangerous Man takes you through a century of Trump family history and exposes key characters in the molding of Donald Trump, his notoriety, his financial empire, and his personality.

About Mary L. Trump

Mary Lea Trump is an American psychologist, businessperson, and author. She is the daughter of Frederick Trump, Jr. and Linda Lee Clapp. She has an English Literature degree from Tufts University, earned a master's degree in English Literature at Columbia University, and holds a Ph.D. in clinical psychology from Adelphi University. Trump was a contributor to the book *Diagnosis: Schizophrenia*, published by Columbia University Press in 2002. She has also taught graduate courses in developmental psychology, trauma, and psychopathology.

In *Too Much and Never Enough: How My Family Created the World's Most Dangerous Man*, Mary L. Trump attempts to expose the dark history of her family in order to explain how her uncle became the man who, she believes, now threatens the world's health, economic security, and social structure.

Trivia Questions

Too Much and Never Enough

1. How many parts are there in the book?
2. What is the name of each part?
3. Who is the first-born son of Fred Trump?
4. What event took place between Freddy and Donald that became a family legend?
5. What airline did Freddy work for?
6. What was Freddy addicted to?
7. What military school did Donald attend?
8. What did Fred think of Freddy's career as a pilot?
9. What kind of sickness afflicted Fred Trump?
10. What newspaper company—with Mary's assistance—exposed a long litany of potentially fraudulent and criminal activities made by the Trump family?

11. Where did Donald decide to go into the casino business?

Mary L. Trump

1. Where did Mary complete her bachelor's degree in Literature?

2. What 2002 publication did Mary contribute to?

3. Who is Mary's mother?

4. Where did Mary complete her Ph.D.?

5. How is Mary related to Donald J. Trump?

6. What type of graduate courses did Mary teach?

7. Where did Mary complete her master's degree in Literature?

Congratulations
on finishing this book!

We hope that you have found this summary **valuable** and had an **enjoyable reading experience**.

We always **strive to improve** ourselves to **deliver the highest quality of work** to you.

But **we cannot improve without you**. If you like our efforts, **please support us** by giving us a quick review of the summary in our Amazon page by visiting the link or by scanning the QR code below. Your support will allow us to produce products of even **better quality** in the future.

https://link.intensivelife.com/TMNESummary

Thank you!

The Intensive Life Publishing Team

About Intensive Life Publishing

We live in a fast-paced world; everyone is always doing something. We started *Intensive Life Publishing* so that we can help people **get key ideas fast**. Our mission is to provide you with **accurate, well-written summaries** of some of the world's best-selling books so that you, as our reader, can **get the valuable information that you need**. This also, in turn, promotes those fantastic, best-selling books and their respective authors.

To know more about Intensive Life Publishing, you can visit **intensivelife.com** and **follow us** on social media:

 @intensivelifepublishing

@intensive_life

Made in the USA
Monee, IL
26 April 2021